Prediction Markets: Investing, Speculation, or Gambling?

Roggie Clark

Continue Learning At Our Website: Roggieclarkbooks.com

Continue exploring educational resources, tools, books, workbooks, and learning materials designed to help readers continue building knowledge and practical skills. Visit: www.roggieclarkbooks.com

Inside you'll find:

- Educational worksheets
- Beginner-friendly guides
- Printable activities
- Companion materials for books and courses

A growing library of educational content for readers, collectors, learners, parents, teachers, and lifelong students.

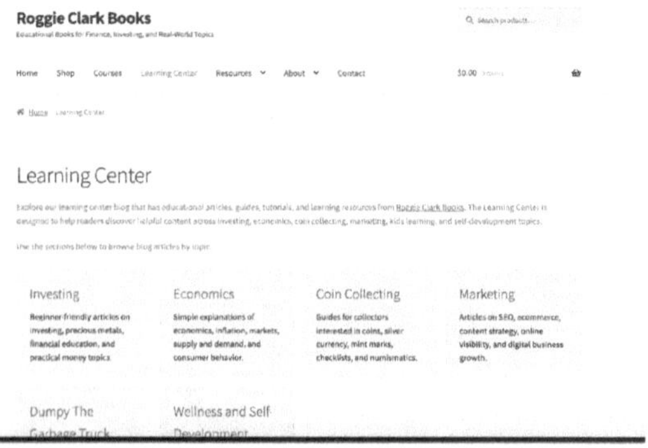

The Strategic Guide to U.S. Mint Gold and Silver Coin Investing

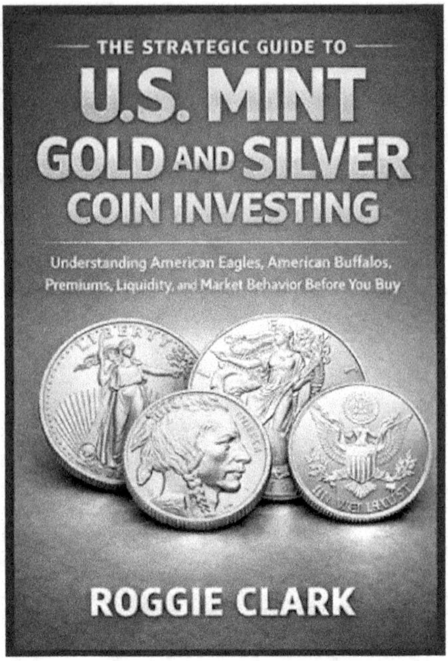

Rather than offering a general introduction to precious metals, this guide examines how American Gold Eagles, American Gold Buffalos, and Silver American Eagles behave in real investor markets.

https://www.amazon.com/Strategic-Guide-U-S-Silver-Investing/dp/B0GQKJF9K6

Copyright

Title: Prediction Markets: Investing, Speculation, or Gambling?
Author: Roggie Clark

Cover Design: Roggie Clark
Editing: Renee' Clark

Printed in the United States of America

Disclaimer

The views and opinions expressed in this publication are those of the author and do not necessarily reflect the official policies, positions, opinions, or viewpoints of any individual, company, organization, institution, agency, or entity referenced or mentioned within this work.

The author is not necessarily affiliated with, endorsed by, sponsored by, or compensated by any individuals, companies, organizations, brands, institutions, products, or services referenced within this publication unless specifically stated otherwise. Any examples, sample situations, stories, illustrations, or scenarios presented may be fictionalized or simplified for educational purposes. Any resemblance to actual persons, living or dead, businesses, or events is purely coincidental unless otherwise stated.

The information, ideas, strategies, concepts, techniques, opinions, suggestions, and educational materials contained in this publication are provided on an "as is" basis without warranties of any kind, either express or implied. While every effort has been made to provide accurate and current information, neither the author nor the publisher makes any representations or warranties regarding the completeness, accuracy, reliability, suitability, or applicability of the information presented.

This publication is intended solely for educational and informational purposes and should not be interpreted as professional advice of any kind, including but not limited to financial, investment, legal, tax, business, medical, mental health, educational, psychological, or other professional guidance. Readers should conduct their own independent research and consult appropriately qualified professionals before making decisions that may affect their finances, health, business, education, legal matters, personal circumstances, or other important areas of life.

Results, outcomes, and experiences may vary significantly among individuals. Neither the author nor the publisher guarantees any specific outcomes, results, earnings, performance improvements, personal achievements, or benefits resulting from the use of information contained in this publication.

By reading, accessing, or using this publication, you acknowledge and agree that the author and publisher shall not be held liable for any direct, indirect, incidental, consequential, financial, personal, emotional, or other damages, losses, or claims arising from the use, misuse, interpretation, or application of information contained within this publication. You assume full responsibility for any actions, decisions, and outcomes resulting from the use of this material.

Image Credits and Public Domain Notice

All images, illustrations, graphics, photographs, visual references, and related materials included in this publication are believed to be in the public domain, used under applicable licenses or permissions, created by the author or publisher, or obtained from sources that clearly identify them as available for lawful use.

The author and publisher have made a good faith effort to use only visual materials that are lawfully available for use and distribution. Where applicable, images and visual materials may have been resized, cropped, edited, enhanced, stylized, modified, reformatted, or arranged for educational, informational, design, formatting, or presentation purposes.

This publication is intended for educational, informational, and illustrative purposes only. The inclusion of any image, artwork, photograph, visual reference, symbol, historical material, design, or graphic element is not intended to claim ownership over public domain materials or any third-party intellectual property rights that remain with their respective owners.

If you believe any image or visual material included in this publication has been used in error, please contact the author or publisher so the matter may be reviewed and corrected in future editions or releases if necessary.

Any factual information, specifications, historical references, values, descriptions, statistics, or related content accompanying visual materials are provided for general informational purposes only and may change over time. Readers should conduct their own independent research and consult appropriate sources or qualified professionals when making decisions based on information presented in this publication.

This publication is independently produced and is not affiliated with, endorsed by, sponsored by, or associated with any company, organization, government agency, institution, trademark holder, or third party unless specifically stated otherwise.

Table of Contents

Introduction: Prediction Markets Are Having a Moment

Prediction markets have moved from being a relatively obscure concept to something that many everyday people are beginning to encounter online. You may see a market asking whether a political candidate will win an election, whether an economic statistic will reach a certain level, whether a sporting event will have a particular result, or whether some other measurable event will occur by a specific date. Instead of simply discussing what they think will happen, participants can put money behind their predictions. That makes prediction markets fascinating, but it also creates an important financial question. When you buy one of these contracts, **what are you actually doing with your money?**

That question is more complicated than it might initially appear. Prediction markets borrow characteristics from several familiar activities. They have prices that rise and fall, much like financial markets. Participants can research information and search for opportunities where they believe a market is incorrectly priced. At the same time, the financial result may depend entirely on whether an uncertain event occurs, which creates obvious similarities to betting. Understanding prediction markets therefore requires more than learning how to click "yes" or "no" on an event. It requires understanding what these markets are designed to accomplish and what risks you accept when you participate.

This book will take that approach from the beginning. It is not built around the assumption that prediction markets are a great investment opportunity, nor will it automatically dismiss them as nothing more than gambling. Instead, we will examine how the markets work, why people participate, how money can be made or lost, and whether putting money into an event contract makes financial sense in the first place.

Why Prediction Markets Are Attracting New Attention

A **prediction market** is a market built around uncertain future events. Participants trade contracts whose value depends on a specified outcome. Rather than purchasing ownership in a company or lending money to an organization, you are taking a financial position on whether something will happen.

That concept is not entirely new. People have long tried to use markets, surveys, betting activity, and other methods to understand expectations about the future. What has changed is how accessible event-based markets can feel to ordinary users. An idea that once sounded like something primarily discussed by economists, researchers, professional traders, or political forecasters can now resemble the familiar experience of using an online financial platform.

Imagine a hypothetical market asking:

Will Country A report inflation above 4 percent in December?

The market could offer contracts tied to "Yes" and "No." Participants who believe inflation will exceed the stated level might take the Yes side. Others might believe the market is overestimating that possibility and take the No side.

Money changes the nature of the prediction. Saying that you are 90 percent certain something will happen in a conversation costs you nothing if you are wrong. Taking a financial position based on that belief forces you to accept consequences if your assessment turns out to be incorrect.

This is one reason prediction markets are interesting beyond their potential for making money. They can provide a way to observe **collective expectations**. As participants buy and sell contracts, their differing beliefs, research, information, and willingness to risk money contribute to the market price.

That does not mean the market possesses some special ability to see the future. Prediction markets can be wrong. Participants can misunderstand information, become overly confident, react emotionally, follow the crowd, or simply encounter an outcome that was difficult to foresee.

The important distinction is that a prediction market attempts to convert different beliefs about uncertainty into a price.

This has helped make prediction markets appealing to several different groups. Someone interested in economics may watch them to see what participants expect from an upcoming announcement. Someone interested in politics may follow election-related markets. A trader may look for prices they believe do not accurately reflect the likelihood of an outcome. Another person may participate primarily because predicting events is entertaining.

Those motivations are not the same, and that distinction will become increasingly important throughout this book.

The Basic Idea Behind Putting Money on Future Outcomes

At the most basic level, a prediction market asks participants to take a position on an outcome that has not happened yet.

Suppose a hypothetical event contract asks:

Will unemployment be below 5 percent on a specified government report date?

There must be clearly defined rules determining what counts as Yes and what counts as No. There must also be an agreed-upon source used to determine the final result. If the stated condition is satisfied, contracts associated with the correct outcome settle according to the market's rules. Contracts associated with the incorrect outcome do not receive the winning payout.

This is where **event contracts** become important. An event contract is not the same thing as buying a share of stock.

When you purchase stock, you are generally purchasing an ownership interest in a company. The company can continue operating for years or decades. Its value can be influenced by revenue, profits, assets, growth expectations, competitive conditions, and many other factors.

An event contract is built around a defined question and resolution.

The event happens, the contract is settled according to its terms, and that particular market reaches an end.

This creates a very different relationship between your money and the asset you are purchasing.

If you put $100 into a traditional investment, you may be thinking about what that asset could be worth five, ten, or twenty years from now. If you put money into an event contract that settles next Tuesday, your financial outcome may be determined next Tuesday.

That difference matters.

Prediction markets can still involve analysis. A participant might study economic data, historical patterns, public information, polling, weather forecasts, industry developments, or other relevant evidence before taking a position. A person could spend considerably more time researching a prediction market than another person spends researching a stock.

But **research effort does not determine whether something is an investment**.

Someone can research a sporting event for twenty hours before placing a wager. Another person can purchase an index fund after ten minutes of research. The amount of work involved does not automatically define the underlying financial activity.

Instead, we need to examine what is being purchased, what produces the potential return, what risks are being taken, and what must happen for the participant to make money.

This is also why the phrase "putting money on future outcomes" should not automatically be interpreted negatively or positively. Prediction markets have legitimate uses beyond someone simply hoping to win money. They can help aggregate expectations, provide information about how participants view uncertain events, and in some circumstances may be used to offset exposure to a particular outcome.

At the same time, none of those uses eliminates financial risk for the person trading the contract.

You can understand the purpose of a market and still lose money participating in it.

The Question This Book Will Answer: Investing, Speculation, or Gambling?

Now we arrive at the central question of this book.

Are prediction markets investing, speculation, or gambling?

There is a temptation to choose one label immediately. Doing so would make the subject easier to explain, but it would also remove much of the nuance that makes prediction markets worth understanding.

Traditional **investing** generally involves committing capital to an asset or enterprise with an expectation of generating a financial return over time. **Speculation** typically places greater emphasis on attempting to profit from changes in price or uncertain future conditions. **Gambling** generally involves risking something of value on an uncertain event in hopes of receiving something of greater value if the outcome is favorable.

Prediction markets can contain characteristics that resemble more than one of these activities.

Consider someone who spends hours studying economic data and concludes that a contract implying a particular probability is incorrectly priced. The person buys the contract because their research suggests the actual probability is higher.

That sounds a lot like speculation based on analysis.

Now consider someone who knows almost nothing about the event but buys a contract because they have a feeling that their preferred outcome will happen.

That looks considerably more like wagering.

Then consider a business owner whose income could be negatively affected by a particular event. If an appropriate legal market exists and the person takes a position that could partially offset the financial damage caused by that event, the purpose begins to resemble **hedging**.

The contract may be similar, but the reason for using it can be completely different.

This is why we should be careful about calling every prediction market participant an "investor." The word can make an activity sound as though it automatically belongs alongside long-term wealth-building strategies. Prediction markets do not necessarily function that way.

A winning event contract also does not create productive value simply because it generated a return for its holder. If you buy a contract at one price and receive a larger payout when the event resolves in your favor, you made money. That fact alone does not answer whether the activity should be considered investing.

Throughout this book, we will therefore separate **how prediction markets work** from **whether participating in them is financially worthwhile**.

Those are two different questions.

You may finish this book fascinated by prediction markets while deciding that you have no interest in putting money into them. You may conclude that they are useful primarily as forecasting tools. You may view certain participation as speculation. You may decide that some forms feel indistinguishable from gambling. Or you may determine that particular uses serve a legitimate financial purpose for certain participants.

The objective is not to force one conclusion.

The objective is to give you enough understanding to reach your own conclusion without relying on marketing language, hype, or the assumption that something becomes an investment simply because it is traded through a market.

Last Thoughts

Prediction markets sit at an unusual intersection of **finance, probability, forecasting, speculation, and wagering**. That intersection is exactly what makes them worth examining carefully. Before deciding whether there is any reason to risk money in these markets, you first need to understand what the contracts represent, how their prices work, and what actually determines whether you make or lose money. In the next chapter, we will begin with those mechanics and break down how prediction markets actually work from the ground up.

Chapter 1: How Prediction Markets Actually Work

Once you understand the basic idea behind prediction markets, the next step is understanding what actually happens when money enters one. The interface can make the process look almost too simple. You see a question, choose a side, decide how much money to risk, and wait to see what happens. Underneath that simplicity, however, is a market with contracts, prices, buyers, sellers, settlement rules, and real financial consequences. Understanding these mechanics is important because prediction markets can feel much more familiar than they actually are. A price displayed as 62 cents may look like the price of an inexpensive asset, but what you are purchasing, how it gains value, and what eventually happens to your money are very different from what occurs with many traditional investments.

Prediction Markets and the Basic Structure of Event-Based Trading

Every prediction market begins with a **specific future outcome** that can eventually be determined.

The question might involve an election, an economic report, a sporting event, a weather measurement, a government decision, or another event that can be objectively resolved. The important part is that the market needs a clear way to determine what happened.

Consider a hypothetical market asking:

Will the unemployment rate be below 4 percent in the December employment report?

There are two possible answers: Yes or No.

Someone who believes the condition will be met can take the Yes side. Someone who believes it will not be met can take the No side.

At first glance, this seems like nothing more than making a prediction. The financial component changes that. Participants are not merely submitting opinions. They are purchasing positions whose financial value depends on the outcome.

That creates a market.

Different participants may have different estimates of how likely the event is to happen. One person might believe there is a 70 percent chance. Another might estimate 50 percent. Someone else may think the probability is only 30 percent.

Those disagreements are important because markets need people willing to take different sides.

Participants may also change their minds as circumstances change.

Suppose several months remain before the hypothetical unemployment contract is resolved. A new economic report is released showing unexpected weakness in the labor market. Participants may interpret that information as making unemployment below 4 percent less likely.

People willing to pay the previous price for Yes contracts may disappear. Others may become more interested in the No side.

The market price can respond.

This is one of the features that separates a prediction market from simply asking a group of people what they believe will happen. A survey might tell you that 60 percent of respondents believe an event will occur. A prediction market produces a price based on actual trading activity among participants willing to put money behind their expectations.

That does not automatically make the market correct.

A large number of participants can reach the wrong conclusion. Traders can overreact to news. Important information can be misunderstood. A market with relatively few participants can behave differently from one with substantial activity.

Unexpected events can completely change what ultimately happens.

The market is therefore not a crystal ball.

It is better understood as a continuously changing financial representation of what market participants are willing to pay for exposure to a particular outcome.

Another important feature is that the underlying question needs to be specific.

A market asking:

"Will the economy be good next year?"

would create an obvious problem. What exactly does "good" mean?

A stronger market would use an objectively measurable condition, such as whether a particular economic statistic will be above or below a specified number on a specified date.

The wording matters because real money depends on the result.

Participants need to know exactly what determines the winner, what information source will be used, what date matters, and what happens if unusual circumstances prevent the event from being resolved normally.

These details may appear less exciting than predicting the outcome itself, but they are part of understanding what you are purchasing.

You are not simply betting on your interpretation of a headline.

You are taking a position on the specific outcome defined by the contract.

Event Contracts, Yes-or-No Outcomes, Prices, and Settlement

We introduced event contracts in the Introduction. Now we can look more closely at how they function.

One of the easiest structures to understand is a **binary contract**. Binary simply means that there are two possible outcomes.

Yes or No.

True or False.

Above or Below.

Occurs or Does Not Occur.

Suppose a hypothetical contract asks:

Will a specified economic index close above 5,000 on December 31?

Imagine the Yes contract is trading at $0.65.

That does not mean you are buying an asset that happens to cost 65 cents in the traditional sense. Instead, you are paying for a contract tied to a particular outcome.

For a simplified example, assume a winning contract settles at $1 and a losing contract settles at $0.

If you purchase a Yes contract for $0.65 and the specified condition occurs, the contract settles at $1.

Your gross difference is:

$1.00 - $0.65 = $0.35

If the condition does not occur, the contract settles at $0, meaning the $0.65 you paid for that contract is lost.

This creates an important relationship between **price, potential reward, and risk**.

A contract purchased for $0.10 may offer a much larger potential gain relative to the amount risked than one purchased for $0.90. But there is usually a reason market participants are willing to pay only $0.10 for it. The market currently views that outcome as considerably less likely.

Likewise, paying $0.90 for a contract may appear safer because the market strongly favors that outcome. But if the unexpected occurs, you could risk $0.90 in an attempt to earn the remaining $0.10 before costs.

This is one of the first places where beginners can misunderstand prediction markets.

A high-probability event is not automatically a low-risk way to make easy money.

Imagine repeatedly risking $0.95 to potentially earn $0.05 because an event appears almost certain. You might win many times. But one unexpected loss could erase the profits from numerous successful contracts.

The relationship between probability and price therefore matters enormously, and we will examine it much more closely in Chapter 2.

For now, the important point is that the contract price affects both how much money you risk and how much you can potentially gain.

Prices also do not necessarily remain where they were when you entered the market.

Suppose you purchased a Yes contract at $0.40.

Later, new information makes the outcome appear more likely, and the contract begins trading around $0.70.

Depending on the market structure and its rules, you may not necessarily have to wait until the event occurs. There may be an opportunity to exit the position before settlement.

That introduces another way people can approach these markets.

One participant might purchase a contract because they want to hold it until the final outcome is known. Another might purchase because they believe the market price will move in their favor before the event occurs.

Those are different strategies.

The first focuses primarily on the final event.

The second also focuses on what other market participants may be willing to pay for the contract before settlement.

This starts to resemble trading in other financial markets, but there remains a major difference: the event contract ultimately has a defined resolution.

At some point, the question needs an answer.

The **settlement rules** determine how that answer is established.

If the market concerns an official economic statistic, the rules might specify the government agency whose published number determines the result. If it concerns an election, the rules need to identify the relevant election and the criteria used to determine the winner. If it concerns a sporting event, the rules must explain how postponements, cancellations, ties, or other unusual circumstances are treated.

Participants should understand those rules before committing money.

A person can correctly predict what they believe the spirit of the question means and still misunderstand how the actual contract is written.

In a market involving money, the written rules matter more than assumptions.

What Happens to Your Money When You Win or Lose

The easiest part of prediction markets to understand is also one of the easiest parts to underestimate.

You can lose money.

The fact that a contract may cost less than one dollar can psychologically make the amount seem insignificant. But participants rarely need to purchase only one contract.

Imagine that a contract costs $0.60.

Buying one means risking $0.60.

Buying 100 means committing $60.

Buying 1,000 means committing $600.

The small unit price can disguise the size of the total position if you focus on the price of each contract rather than the amount of money actually exposed to the outcome.

Suppose you purchase 100 hypothetical Yes contracts for $0.60 each.

Your total cost is:

100 x $0.60 = $60

If the contracts settle at $1 because the event occurs, their settlement value would be $100.

Before considering any applicable fees or other costs, the difference between the $100 settlement value and your $60 purchase cost would be $40.

Now consider the opposite outcome.

If Yes is wrong and those contracts settle at $0, the $60 committed to the contracts is lost.

This illustrates an important characteristic of many prediction market positions: **the outcome can be financially unforgiving**.

There is not necessarily an underlying company, piece of property, bond, commodity, or other productive asset remaining after your prediction is wrong.

The contract resolves.

You were either on the financially favorable side of that resolution or you were not.

That does not mean every prediction market trade must be held until settlement. As discussed earlier, some markets may allow positions to be bought and sold before the event resolves. If the market moves in your favor, you might be able to exit at a higher price. If it moves against you, you might choose to exit at a lower price rather than continue holding the position.

But exiting early creates another important reality.

A **paper gain** is not necessarily the same thing as money you have actually secured.

Suppose you purchase a contract for $0.35 and later see it quoted at $0.70. It may appear that your position has doubled in value.

That does not necessarily mean you can instantly sell every contract you own at exactly $0.70.

There must be sufficient market activity on the other side of your transaction. The prices available to buyers and sellers can differ, and the amount you can actually receive may depend on the available orders in the market.

We will explore that problem more deeply when we discuss liquidity and spreads in Chapter 4.

For now, the larger lesson is simple: always think about prediction markets in terms of **money at risk**, not merely the number displayed beside the contract.

If you put $200 into a position, ask yourself what happens to that $200 under different outcomes.

How much can you realistically make?

How much can you lose?

When is the money available again?

What must happen for you to receive the maximum payout?

What happens if you want to exit before the event is resolved?

And perhaps most importantly, are you comfortable with the possibility that your prediction is completely wrong?

That final question matters because people can become emotionally attached to their predictions.

Research can create confidence. Confidence can become certainty. Certainty can encourage someone to risk more money.

But uncertainty does not disappear simply because you have researched an event carefully.

A prediction market exists precisely because the outcome has not been determined yet.

That uncertainty is what creates the opportunity for a financial payoff, but it is also what creates the possibility of a financial loss.

Last Thoughts

Prediction markets become much easier to understand once you stop viewing them as mysterious forecasting systems and start looking at the contracts themselves. There is a defined question, a financial position tied to an outcome, a market price, rules for determining what happened, and money that can be gained or lost depending on the result and how the position is managed. The mechanics may be straightforward, but deciding whether a contract is worth its price is much harder. To answer that question, you need to understand what the price is actually telling you. In the next chapter, we will look at prices, odds, and probabilities, including why an event that is very likely to happen can still be a terrible trade.

Chapter 2: Understanding Prices, Odds, and Probabilities

Seeing a prediction market contract priced at 72 cents can make the market appear straightforward. If the contract pays $1 when the predicted event occurs, it may seem reasonable to interpret that price as the market saying there is roughly a 72 percent chance of the event happening. That interpretation can be useful, but beginners need to understand what sits behind it. Market prices are created by people buying and selling contracts, not by a machine that knows the true probability of the future. A price can reflect available information, changing expectations, disagreement, uncertainty, and sometimes simple human error. More importantly, knowing which outcome is most likely is not enough to determine whether a contract is worth buying. The real question is whether the probability you believe is reasonable justifies the price you are being asked to pay.

How Contract Prices Can Represent Implied Probabilities

One of the most interesting features of prediction markets is the relationship between contract prices and **implied probability**.

Consider a simplified Yes contract trading for $0.60 that settles at $1 if the event occurs and $0 if it does not.

That 60-cent price can commonly be interpreted as the market implying approximately a 60 percent probability of the event occurring.

A contract at $0.25 suggests roughly 25 percent.

A contract at $0.80 suggests roughly 80 percent.

This makes prediction market prices relatively intuitive.

Instead of seeing traditional betting odds or trying to interpret a complicated financial instrument, someone can look at a contract trading around 45 cents and understand that the market is roughly pricing the event as having a 45 percent chance of occurring.

But there is an important word in that sentence:

Roughly.

A market price should not automatically be treated as a scientifically calculated probability.

The price is ultimately the result of market activity. Buyers decide what they are willing to pay. Sellers decide what they are willing to accept. Those decisions collectively create the prices visible in the market.

Suppose a hypothetical contract asks:

Will inflation be below 3 percent in the December report?

Imagine the Yes contract is trading around $0.40.

The simplest interpretation would be that the market is implying approximately a 40 percent probability of that outcome.

Now imagine you have researched inflation trends and believe the actual probability is closer to 55 percent.

That disagreement is where prediction market trading becomes interesting.

You are not necessarily saying:

"I know inflation will be below 3 percent."

You are saying something more specific:

"I believe the probability of this happening is greater than what the current market price appears to imply."

That distinction is extremely important.

Nobody needs to know the future with certainty to participate in a prediction market. Participants are making decisions under uncertainty.

The challenge is determining whether the market has priced that uncertainty appropriately.

Imagine another contract trading at $0.90.

The market is effectively signaling that participants consider the Yes outcome highly likely.

You might agree.

Perhaps you believe there is a 92 percent chance of the event occurring.

But agreement about the likely winner does not automatically mean you should purchase the contract.

You still need to consider the price.

If you pay $0.90 for something that can settle at a maximum of $1, the most you can gain from holding that simplified contract to a successful settlement is $0.10 before considering applicable costs.

The amount you could lose is $0.90.

That trade-off exists because the market already expects the event to happen.

Prediction markets therefore reward more than identifying likely outcomes. The price at which you enter matters.

This is similar to an important principle found throughout financial markets: something can be attractive at one price and unattractive at another.

The prediction itself and the price of the prediction are two different things.

Understanding that distinction is one of the biggest steps a beginner can take toward thinking clearly about these markets.

Why Prices Change When New Information Enters the Market

The future is uncertain, but information about the future is constantly changing.

Prediction market prices can change with it.

Suppose a market asks whether a particular economic measure will exceed a specified level by the end of the year.

Several months before the deadline, the Yes contract trades around $0.45.

Then new economic data is released.

The report strongly suggests that reaching the specified level has become more likely.

Participants react.

Some people who previously favored No may reconsider their positions. Traders who already believed Yes was underpriced may become willing to pay more. New participants may enter after seeing the report.

As buying and selling behavior changes, the market price may rise from $0.45 to $0.60, $0.70, or another level.

The event has not happened yet.

What changed was the information available to participants and their interpretation of that information.

This is sometimes described as **price discovery**, the process through which trading activity contributes to determining the market price of something.

Prediction markets provide an especially interesting example because the thing being priced is uncertainty about a future event.

Information can arrive from many directions.

An election-related market might react to polling, debates, candidate announcements, court decisions, economic conditions, or other developments.

An economic market might react to government reports, central bank announcements, employment data, inflation statistics, or unexpected economic events.

A sports-related market might react to injuries, roster changes, weather conditions, or other information relevant to the event.

The important point is that market prices are not fixed predictions.

They are changing assessments.

A contract trading at $0.70 today could trade at $0.40 tomorrow if important information changes how participants view the event.

This creates both opportunities and risks.

Suppose you purchased the contract at $0.45 because you believed the market was underestimating the probability of Yes.

New information appears to support your view.

The contract rises to $0.70.

Depending on the market's structure, you may be able to sell before settlement and realize a gain rather than waiting for the final outcome.

But the opposite can happen just as easily.

You buy at $0.45.

New information makes the outcome appear considerably less likely.

The contract falls to $0.20.

You now have a decision to make.

Do you continue holding because you still believe your original prediction?

Do you exit and accept a loss?

Was the new information meaningful enough to change your estimate?

Or are other participants overreacting?

These questions demonstrate why prediction markets can quickly become more complicated than simply choosing which outcome you think will happen.

You are not operating in isolation.

Other people are processing the same information.

Some may have more experience than you. Some may have better models. Some may have misunderstood the information. Some may be acting emotionally. Some may simply have a different interpretation.

This leads to the concept of **market efficiency**.

In simple terms, an efficient market is one in which available information is incorporated into prices relatively quickly.

If everyone knows an important piece of information, finding an easy opportunity to profit from it becomes difficult because the market price may already reflect that information.

Imagine a major economic report is released at 8:30 a.m.

You read the report at 10:00 a.m. and discover something you believe makes a particular outcome much more likely.

The problem is that thousands of other people may have seen the same report before you.

If the contract has already moved from $0.40 to $0.75, buying it at $0.75 is a very different proposition from buying it at $0.40.

You may have reached the correct conclusion.

You may simply have reached it too late to obtain an attractive price.

This is another reason being knowledgeable about an event does not automatically translate into making money from it.

Markets do not reward you merely for knowing something.

They reward you when your understanding gives you an advantage relative to the price available when you act.

Why a High Probability Does Not Necessarily Mean a Good Trade

This may be the most important lesson in the chapter:

Likely does not automatically mean profitable.

Suppose a contract is trading at $0.95.

You look at the underlying event and think:

"There is almost no way this loses."

That feeling can make the contract extremely tempting.

After all, if the event appears almost certain, earning five cents on every successful contract might seem like easy money.

But look at the financial relationship more carefully.

In our simplified example, you are risking $0.95 to potentially earn $0.05.

If you purchase 1,000 contracts, you would commit:

1,000 x $0.95 = $950

If the event occurs and the contracts settle at $1, their settlement value would be $1,000.

Your gross gain would be:

$1,000 - $950 = $50

But if the unexpected outcome occurs and the contracts settle at $0, you could lose the $950 committed to the position.

You are potentially risking $950 to make $50.

That does not automatically make the trade bad. If the probability were sufficiently favorable, the mathematics could still justify the position.

But "this seems almost certain" is not enough.

This is where **expected value** becomes useful.

Expected value is a way of thinking about potential outcomes by considering both their probabilities and their financial consequences.

Suppose a Yes contract costs $0.60 and pays $1 if correct.

You estimate that the actual probability of Yes is 70 percent.

Using a simplified framework, the probability-weighted value of the $1 payout would be:

70% x $1 = $0.70

You are being asked to pay $0.60 for something you estimate is worth $0.70 based on your probability assessment.

That suggests a theoretical advantage of $0.10 per contract before considering fees, spreads, taxes, estimation errors, and other practical factors.

Now suppose the same contract costs $0.80.

You still believe there is a 70 percent probability of Yes.

The event has not changed.

Your prediction has not changed.

But the trade has.

You would now be paying $0.80 for something your probability estimate values at $0.70.

Under that simplified framework, the price is no longer attractive.

This demonstrates why prediction markets are not simply about answering:

"What do I think will happen?"

A more useful question is:

"What do I think the probability is, and how does my estimate compare with the price?"

That is considerably harder.

Humans are not naturally perfect probability calculators.

We can become overly confident in outcomes we want to happen. We can give too much weight to recent information. We can mistake something being possible for it being probable. We can also underestimate unlikely events because they feel unrealistic.

Imagine you believe an event has an 80 percent chance of occurring.

You might feel extremely confident.

But an 80 percent probability still implies that the opposite outcome occurs approximately 20 percent of the time if your probability estimate is accurate across comparable situations.

That is roughly one out of five.

Something can therefore be highly likely and still fail.

This becomes especially important when someone repeatedly purchases expensive contracts associated with outcomes they consider "almost guaranteed."

Winning nine times can create a sense of skill and security.

The tenth trade can erase much of that progress if the amount being risked is substantially larger than the potential profit.

Prediction markets can therefore create an unusual psychological trap.

Frequent wins do not necessarily mean someone has a profitable strategy.

A participant could have an extremely high **win rate** while still losing money overall.

Imagine repeatedly risking $90 to make $10.

Nine successful trades generate $90 in total gains.

One complete $90 loss wipes out those gains.

The participant was correct 90 percent of the time and still made no money in this simplified example.

That is why focusing only on how often you are right can be misleading.

What matters is the relationship between how often you are right, how much you make when you are right, and how much you lose when you are wrong.

This brings us back to the larger question of the book.

If you are going to call prediction market participation an investment, you should be able to explain why the expected financial reward justifies putting your capital at risk.

If the reasoning is simply:

"I think this is going to happen,"

you have not yet answered that question.

You have made a prediction.

Whether that prediction represents a financially sensible trade depends on the price.

Last Thoughts

Prediction market prices can make uncertainty easier to visualize, but they should never be confused with certainty itself. A 70-cent contract can suggest that the market considers an outcome relatively likely, yet the market can be wrong, your own probability estimate can be wrong, and even a correct prediction can be purchased at an unattractive price. The central challenge is not simply identifying what you believe will happen. It is determining whether the potential reward justifies the price and the possibility of being wrong. In the next chapter, we will build on this foundation by examining how people actually try to make money in prediction markets, including why correctly predicting an event does not always mean you made a good financial decision.

Chapter 3: How People Try to Make Money

Once prediction market prices are understood as expressions of probability rather than simple price tags, it becomes easier to see how participants try to profit. The basic idea is not necessarily to predict every event correctly. Instead, a participant may look for situations where they believe the market's price does not accurately reflect the likelihood of an outcome. That distinction matters because prediction markets are ultimately markets of disagreement. If everyone agreed about both the outcome and its probability, there would be far fewer reasons to trade. The opportunity, at least in theory, appears when your assessment of an event differs meaningfully from the price available in the market. The difficult part is determining whether you have actually found an opportunity or have simply convinced yourself that you know more than the market does.

Buying Contracts When You Believe the Market Has Mispriced an Outcome

A **mispriced contract** is one that a participant believes is trading at a price that does not accurately reflect the probability of its outcome.

Suppose a hypothetical Yes contract trades for $0.35.

The market price suggests an implied probability of approximately 35 percent.

After examining the available information, you estimate that the event actually has a 55 percent chance of occurring.

If your assessment is reasonable, the contract may appear underpriced.

You are being asked to pay $0.35 for exposure to an outcome that you believe has a considerably greater chance of producing a $1 settlement.

That difference between your probability estimate and the market's price is the reason you might consider buying.

Notice what you are not necessarily saying.

You are not saying:

"This event will definitely happen."

You are saying:

"I believe the market is underestimating how likely this event is to happen."

Those are very different statements.

In fact, you could purchase the contract believing there is only a 55 percent chance of success. You recognize that the event could easily fail to occur. Your argument is simply that 55 percent is sufficiently higher than the roughly 35 percent implied by the price to make the risk potentially attractive.

This introduces the idea of having an **edge**.

An edge is a perceived advantage that makes a participant believe the probabilities are more favorable than the market price suggests.

Where could that advantage come from?

It might come from better analysis.

A participant following an economic market may have studied historical data and developed a stronger understanding of the variables affecting an upcoming report.

Someone trading a sports-related event might believe the market has overreacted to recent results while overlooking longer-term performance.

Another participant may specialize in a narrow subject and believe that their familiarity with it allows them to interpret public information more effectively than less knowledgeable traders.

But there is an uncomfortable question that should accompany every supposed edge:

Why do I think the market is wrong and I am right?

That question is easy to ignore.

Suppose a contract is trading at $0.20 and you believe it should be closer to $0.60.

That appears to be an enormous opportunity.

But before putting money behind that conclusion, you should consider another possibility.

Maybe you are missing something.

Perhaps other participants have considered information you overlooked. Perhaps you misunderstood the contract's settlement rules. Perhaps your probability estimate is being influenced by personal preferences. Perhaps the event seems more likely because you have recently encountered several pieces of information supporting your position.

The existence of disagreement does not prove that you have found mispricing.

Sometimes the market is wrong.

Sometimes you are wrong.

Separating those two situations is where much of the difficulty lies.

This is also why prediction market participation can become dangerous when confidence replaces analysis.

A participant may begin with a reasonable idea:

"I think this contract is slightly underpriced."

After reading more information supporting that position, the thought can gradually become:

"This market is obviously wrong."

Then:

"There is almost no way I lose this."

That progression can encourage someone to increase the amount of money at risk precisely when they should be thinking most carefully about uncertainty.

A strong opinion is not the same thing as a measurable advantage.

There is another way participants may attempt to profit from perceived mispricing.

They may not intend to hold the contract until settlement at all.

Suppose you purchase a contract for $0.30 because you expect an upcoming information release to change market expectations. After the information becomes public, the contract rises to $0.50.

Depending on the market and available buyers, you may be able to sell your position rather than waiting for the underlying event.

In that situation, you attempted to profit from the market's changing assessment rather than solely from the final outcome.

This begins to resemble short-term financial trading.

But the underlying challenge remains the same.

You needed to purchase at a price that ultimately allowed you to sell at a more favorable one.

Simply predicting the direction correctly is not enough if the available prices, transaction costs, or market conditions prevent the trade from being profitable.

Expected Value, Potential Returns, and the Importance of What You Pay

Expected value was introduced in the previous chapter because it provides a useful framework for thinking about prediction market prices. Now we can connect it more directly to how participants attempt to make money.

Consider a simplified contract priced at $0.40.

You estimate that the probability of the contract settling at $1 is 50 percent.

Based on your estimate, the probability-weighted value of the $1 settlement is:

50% x $1 = $0.50

You would be paying $0.40 for something you estimate has a probability-weighted value of $0.50.

The difference is $0.10.

That sounds attractive.

But suppose you are wrong about the probability.

The true probability might be closer to 30 percent.

In that case, you paid $0.40 for an outcome that, under this simplified framework, had a probability-weighted value of only $0.30.

The mathematical framework did not fail.

Your input did.

This is a crucial limitation of expected value calculations.

The arithmetic can be simple.

Estimating the probability is the difficult part.

A calculator can tell you what happens if an event has a 65 percent probability. It cannot necessarily tell you whether your 65 percent estimate is reasonable.

This is where prediction markets can create a false sense of precision.

Someone may say:

"I estimate a 72 percent probability."

The number sounds sophisticated.

But where did 72 percent come from?

Was it generated by a tested statistical model?

Was it based on historical data?

Was it derived from several independent pieces of evidence?

Or did the person simply think the event felt "pretty likely" and assign it a number?

Putting a percentage on an opinion does not automatically make the opinion more accurate.

This matters because relatively small probability errors can completely change whether a trade appears attractive.

Suppose a contract costs $0.65.

You estimate the event has a 75 percent chance of occurring.

That appears favorable.

But if your estimate should actually have been 60 percent, the same contract looks very different.

The price never changed.

Your understanding of the probability did.

This is why **entry price** deserves so much attention.

Imagine that you believe an event has a 70 percent probability of occurring.

At $0.40, you may consider the contract extremely attractive.

At $0.60, you may still find it attractive.

At $0.69, the potential advantage becomes very small.

At $0.80, you might decide that the price is too high despite still believing the event is more likely to happen than not.

The event itself did not change in this example.

Only the price changed.

This demonstrates why the phrase "I think Yes will win" is incomplete from a financial perspective.

At what price?

That question is essential.

A participant who ignores price can be correct about an event while still taking an unattractive risk.

Potential returns also need to be considered in relation to potential losses.

Suppose you purchase 100 contracts at $0.80.

Your total cost is $80.

If the contracts settle at $1, their settlement value is $100.

Your gross gain is $20 before applicable costs.

If the contracts settle at $0, you lose the $80 committed to them.

The question is not simply whether $20 sounds worthwhile.

The question is whether the probability of earning that $20 sufficiently compensates you for the possibility of losing $80.

This is the same reason a contract priced at $0.10 should not automatically be viewed as a bargain.

Yes, the potential percentage gain can be enormous if it settles at $1.

But the low price may reflect a very low probability of that happening.

Cheap does not automatically mean undervalued.

Expensive does not automatically mean safe.

The relationship among probability, price, potential gain, and potential loss is what matters.

And even then, the calculation is incomplete if it ignores practical costs such as fees, spreads, taxes, or difficulty exiting a position. We will examine some of those issues more closely in the next chapter.

Why Being Right About an Event Does Not Always Mean You Made a Good Financial Decision

Prediction markets create a strange relationship between being right and making a good decision.

Those two things can overlap.

They are not identical.

Imagine that someone purchases a Yes contract for $0.98.

The contract settles at $1.

The participant was correct.

They earned $0.02 per contract before applicable costs.

Now imagine that the participant had no meaningful analysis supporting the position. They simply believed the outcome was "basically guaranteed" and risked a large amount of money to capture the remaining two cents.

The event happened.

The trade made money.

Was it a good financial decision?

You cannot answer that question solely from the result.

This introduces an important distinction between **outcome quality and decision quality**.

Outcome quality asks:

What happened?

Decision quality asks:

Was the decision reasonable based on the information, probabilities, risks, and potential rewards available when it was made?

A poor decision can produce a good outcome.

A good decision can produce a bad outcome.

Suppose you estimate that an event has a 70 percent probability of occurring and find a contract available at $0.30.

Your analysis is careful. Your reasoning is sound. The price appears attractive relative to your probability estimate.

You purchase the contract.

The event does not happen.

You lose.

That loss does not automatically prove the original decision was foolish.

If an event truly has a 70 percent probability, it still fails to occur 30 percent of the time.

Uncertainty means reasonable decisions sometimes produce losses.

Now consider the opposite situation.

Someone puts nearly all of their available cash into a highly uncertain contract because they have a feeling about the outcome.

They win.

The successful result does not automatically transform the original decision into responsible financial behavior.

This distinction matters because prediction markets can provide extremely fast emotional feedback.

You make a prediction.

You risk money.

You find out whether you were right.

A win can create confidence.

Several wins can create much more confidence.

Soon, a participant may begin believing that successful outcomes prove they possess exceptional forecasting ability.

This is where **resulting**, judging the quality of a decision primarily by its outcome, can become dangerous.

Imagine someone makes five poorly researched predictions and happens to win four.

They may conclude:

"I am good at prediction markets."

Another participant makes five carefully researched trades with favorable expected value and happens to lose three.

They may conclude:

"I am terrible at this."

Neither conclusion necessarily follows from such a small collection of outcomes.

Randomness matters.

Probability matters.

Sample size matters.

The quality of the original decisions matters.

This is especially important because the consequences of being wrong are not always equal.

Suppose one participant makes ten trades.

Nine generate $10 each.

One loses $200.

The participant was right nine times out of ten.

They still lost $110 overall.

A 90 percent win rate sounds impressive until the size of the losses is considered.

This is why evaluating prediction market performance requires more than counting wins.

You need to know how much money was risked, how much was earned when positions succeeded, how much was lost when they failed, and whether the decisions were based on a repeatable advantage or fortunate outcomes.

There is also an important opportunity-cost question.

Suppose someone spends hundreds of hours researching event contracts over the course of a year and earns $300.

Technically, they made money.

But was prediction market participation the best use of that time and capital?

Could the money have served a more useful purpose elsewhere?

Could those hundreds of hours have produced greater value through work, a business, education, or another activity?

These questions become particularly relevant when prediction markets are presented as an "investment opportunity."

Making money from something does not automatically make it a good investment.

Someone can make money buying collectibles, reselling concert tickets, playing poker, flipping merchandise, trading financial assets, or participating in prediction markets.

The existence of profit does not tell us whether the activity is appropriate for a particular person's financial goals.

That is why the point of this book is not to teach you how to find a "winning prediction."

The more important skill is learning how to evaluate the financial decision surrounding the prediction.

Before putting money into a contract, you should be able to explain what you believe the probability is, why you believe the market price is wrong, how much you could realistically gain, how much you could lose, and why the potential reward justifies taking that risk.

If the entire argument is:

"I just know this is going to happen,"

you may have a prediction.

You do not necessarily have an edge.

Last Thoughts

People try to make money in prediction markets by identifying situations where they believe the available price does not accurately reflect the probability of an outcome. In theory, consistently finding those differences can create profitable opportunities. In practice, the hardest part is determining whether the market is actually mispriced or whether your own probability estimate is wrong. Even successful predictions can hide poor financial decisions when the potential gain is small compared with the amount being risked. Understanding potential profit therefore requires understanding potential loss. In the next chapter, we will examine the risks that are easy to overlook, including liquidity, spreads, fees, bad information, emotional decision-making, and the way many seemingly small trades can quietly create much larger financial exposure.

Chapter 4: The Risks That Are Easy to Overlook

The possibility of losing a prediction is obvious. If you buy a contract tied to an outcome and that outcome does not occur, you can lose the money committed to the position. But that is only one part of the risk. Prediction markets contain less obvious risks that can affect returns even when your reasoning about an event is fairly good. You may have trouble exiting at the price you expected, transaction costs can reduce a seemingly attractive opportunity, new information can completely change the market, and confidence can encourage you to risk more money than originally intended. Perhaps most importantly, the small price of individual contracts can make it surprisingly easy to build substantial financial exposure without fully appreciating how much money is at stake.

Liquidity, Spreads, Fees, and the Realities of Entering and Exiting Positions

A contract might display a price of $0.55 on your screen, but that does not necessarily mean you can buy or sell any quantity you want at exactly $0.55.

One reason is **liquidity**.

Liquidity describes how easily something can be bought or sold without substantially affecting its price. A market with many active participants and many available orders may have relatively strong liquidity. A market with few participants and limited trading activity may have poor liquidity.

This difference matters when real money is involved.

Suppose you purchase 100 contracts at $0.40.

Later, the market moves in your favor and the displayed price reaches approximately $0.70.

On paper, the position appears to have gained substantially.

It can be tempting to calculate:

$0.70 - $0.40 = $0.30 profit per contract.

But you still need someone willing to purchase your contracts.

Perhaps buyers are willing to purchase only 20 contracts near $0.70. Additional buyers may be offering $0.68, $0.65, or lower prices.

Selling all 100 contracts could therefore produce a different result from simply multiplying 100 by the price displayed on the screen.

This is where **market depth** becomes important.

Market depth refers to the quantity of orders available at different prices. A market may look active because contracts are changing hands, but there may not be enough orders near the current price to accommodate a large transaction.

For someone trading only a few dollars, this may be less noticeable.

As the size of a position increases, it can become considerably more important.

Another cost comes from the **bid-ask spread**.

The bid represents what buyers are currently willing to pay. The ask represents what sellers are currently willing to accept.

Suppose buyers are offering $0.48 while sellers are asking $0.52.

The four-cent difference is the spread.

If you want to enter or exit immediately, that difference can affect the economics of your trade.

Imagine buying at $0.52 and immediately deciding to sell. If the best available buyer is offering only $0.48, you could take a loss even though nothing about the underlying event has changed.

The prediction did not go against you.

The market did not receive surprising news.

You simply crossed the spread.

This can be especially important in markets with limited activity. Wider spreads make it more expensive to move quickly in and out of positions.

Then there are **transaction fees** and other costs.

The exact costs depend on the market and the rules under which someone participates. A platform may charge fees associated with transactions, withdrawals, settlement, or other activities.

Even small costs can matter when the expected profit from a contract is small.

Consider someone purchasing a contract for $0.94 because they believe it is highly likely to settle at $1.

The maximum gross difference is only $0.06 per contract.

If various transaction costs consume part of that six cents, the actual return becomes smaller.

The participant might correctly predict the outcome and still earn considerably less than the simple contract price initially suggested.

This is why **gross profit and net profit** should be treated differently.

Gross profit is what the trade appears to earn before relevant costs.

Net profit is what remains after those costs.

The distinction is basic, but it becomes important when prediction market opportunities involve relatively small potential gains.

Liquidity can also become especially important when circumstances suddenly change.

Imagine that you own a large position in a contract.

Breaking news appears that dramatically weakens your prediction.

You decide to sell immediately.

Unfortunately, many other participants have reached the same conclusion.

Buyers disappear.

Prices fall rapidly.

The price you expected to receive may no longer be available.

This is **exit risk**.

It is easy to imagine entering a position because you control when you purchase it. It is more dangerous to assume you will always be able to leave the position exactly when and how you want.

Markets do not guarantee convenient exits.

That reality should be considered before the position is opened, not after something goes wrong.

Uncertainty, Bad Information, Emotional Decisions, and Overconfidence

Every prediction market is built around uncertainty.

If the outcome were already known with certainty, there would be little reason for a prediction market to exist.

The challenge is that people are often uncomfortable with uncertainty.

We naturally look for patterns, explanations, and information that make the future feel more predictable. Research can help, but it can also create an illusion of control.

The more information someone collects, the easier it can become to believe that uncertainty has disappeared.

It has not.

Suppose you spend several hours researching an economic event.

You read reports.

You examine historical data.

You listen to analysts.

You compare several forecasts.

Eventually, you become convinced that Yes is the correct position.

Research may have improved your estimate.

But the event remains uncertain.

There could be information you have not seen. Your sources could be wrong. The historical relationship you identified might not continue. An unexpected event could occur before settlement.

Even accurate information can be interpreted incorrectly.

Then there is the problem of **information quality**.

Prediction markets can involve fast-moving events, particularly when participants are reacting to news.

In that environment, rumors can spread quickly.

A social media post may be mistaken for confirmed information. An old article may be shared as though it were new. A statistic may be removed from its original context. Someone with a large online following may make a confident prediction without providing meaningful evidence.

If money is already at risk, participants can become especially vulnerable to information that supports what they want to believe.

This is known as **confirmation bias**.

Confirmation bias is the tendency to give greater attention or importance to information that supports an existing belief while discounting information that challenges it.

Suppose you own Yes contracts.

A positive report appears.

You immediately think:

"I knew I was right."

Then a negative report appears.

You respond:

"That probably does not matter."

The danger is obvious.

You are no longer evaluating information neutrally. You are evaluating it through the position you already own.

Money can intensify that tendency.

Selling the contract may require admitting that your original reasoning was wrong. Holding it allows you to continue hoping that the market will eventually prove you correct.

This can turn analysis into emotional attachment.

Another problem is **overconfidence**.

A participant who successfully predicts several events may begin believing that their success proves exceptional forecasting ability.

Perhaps it does.

But perhaps they were fortunate.

A short winning streak does not provide enough information to distinguish skill from randomness.

This can lead to a dangerous cycle.

A person starts with $10 positions.

They win several.

They increase to $25.

They continue winning.

Now they risk $100.

Then $500.

The person's forecasting ability may not have improved at all.

Only the amount being risked changed.

Overconfidence can also encourage people to concentrate too much money in a single prediction.

A person might think:

"I normally risk $50, but I am so sure about this one that I am putting in $1,000."

That sentence should immediately raise a question.

If the event is uncertain, why has confidence justified increasing the potential damage of being wrong twentyfold?

Confidence does not reduce the size of the financial loss if the outcome goes against you.

Emotion can create other problems as well.

After losing money, someone may feel an urge to recover it quickly. Instead of stopping and reconsidering their decisions, they may immediately take another position.

This behavior is often called **chasing losses**.

Suppose someone loses $200.

They become frustrated.

A new market appears.

Normally they would risk $25, but they decide to risk $200 because a successful trade could recover the previous loss.

Now the size of the new position is being determined by an emotional reaction to an unrelated outcome.

The market does not know that you lost $200 earlier.

It does not owe the money back to you.

Each new contract has its own probabilities, price, and risks.

Trying to force the next trade to repair the previous one can turn a manageable loss into a much larger financial problem.

Why Repeated Small Trades Can Create Much Larger Financial Exposure Than Expected

Prediction markets can feel inexpensive because individual contracts may trade for amounts such as $0.20, $0.50, or $0.80.

Those numbers do not look intimidating.

But the price of one contract is not the same thing as the size of your financial exposure.

Consider someone who purchases 200 contracts at $0.50.

That is:

200 x $0.50 = $100

Now suppose they also purchase $75 worth of contracts in another market.

Then $50 in another.

Then $125 in another.

Then another $100.

Each decision may feel relatively small when considered individually.

Together, the participant now has $450 committed across several predictions.

This is **aggregate exposure**, the total amount of financial risk created by multiple positions considered together.

Looking only at individual trades can hide this larger picture.

A person may tell themselves:

"I never risk more than $100 on a prediction."

That sounds controlled.

But if they have ten $100 positions open simultaneously, the more important number may be $1,000.

There is another complication.

Different contracts may appear unrelated while actually depending on similar underlying events.

Suppose someone owns several contracts tied to inflation, interest rates, employment, and economic growth.

These are technically different questions.

But economic developments can influence several of them at the same time.

A single unexpected economic event could therefore hurt multiple positions.

This creates **correlated risk**.

Diversification only helps when the risks are sufficiently different.

Owning ten contracts does not necessarily provide meaningful diversification if all ten are vulnerable to the same underlying development.

Political markets can create similar situations.

Someone may hold contracts concerning an election winner, control of a legislative body, voter turnout, and several related political outcomes.

They may think they have four separate predictions.

In reality, the positions could be heavily connected.

If one major political development changes expectations, several contracts might move against the participant simultaneously.

Repeated trading also creates a behavioral risk.

A $10 trade may feel insignificant.

That can make it easier to place another.

And another.

And another.

Imagine someone makes five $10 trades during the morning.

Another five in the afternoon.

Then several more in the evening.

No single decision feels particularly serious.

But over time, the total amount of money moving through the account can become substantial.

This is one reason frequency matters.

Small stakes do not automatically mean small financial consequences when the activity is repeated often enough.

The same issue can appear with profits.

Suppose someone wins $40 and immediately treats that money as though it does not count because it came from the market.

They use the $40 to take another position.

Then another.

This is sometimes called the **house money effect**, the tendency to become more willing to take risks with money that was recently won.

But money does not become less real because it came from a successful prediction.

Once you have earned $40, it is your $40.

Risking it again is a new financial decision.

This is another reason prediction markets can begin feeling more like entertainment than financial decision-making.

When the numbers on the screen stop feeling like actual money, risk becomes easier to underestimate.

A useful way to counter this is to think in dollar terms rather than contracts.

Do not think:

"I have 500 contracts."

Think:

"I currently have $300 that could be affected by this outcome."

Do not think:

"I am only buying another 100."

Think:

"I am committing another $65."

That shift keeps the financial consequences visible.

It also brings us back to the question at the center of this book.

If prediction markets are being treated as investments, the amount of capital committed to them should matter.

If they are being treated as speculation, the amount of speculative exposure should matter.

And if they are being used primarily for entertainment, the amount of money someone is willing to lose for that entertainment should matter.

Changing the label does not change the dollars at risk.

Last Thoughts

The most obvious prediction market risk is choosing the wrong outcome, but many losses can be influenced by problems that exist around the prediction itself. Limited liquidity can make positions difficult to exit, spreads and fees can reduce returns, poor information can distort decisions, and overconfidence can turn reasonable position sizes into dangerous ones. Repeated small trades can also create far more financial exposure than any individual trade appears to represent. These risks make the central question of this book even more important. If money is being exposed to uncertain outcomes in pursuit of a financial return, what exactly should we call that activity? In the next chapter, we will directly compare prediction markets with traditional investing, financial speculation, sportsbooks, and gambling to determine where prediction markets actually fit.

Chapter 5: Investing, Speculation, or Gambling?

Prediction markets become difficult to categorize because they borrow characteristics from several financial activities at once. They have tradable contracts and changing market prices, which can make them resemble financial markets. Participants may conduct research, estimate probabilities, and search for mispriced opportunities, which can resemble speculation. Yet the ultimate value of many contracts depends on whether a defined uncertain event occurs, creating an obvious resemblance to wagering. Rather than forcing every prediction market transaction into one category, it is more useful to examine what the participant owns, where the potential return comes from, how the risk is structured, and why the person is putting money into the market in the first place.

What Prediction Markets Share With Traditional Investing and Financial Trading

Prediction markets can look surprisingly similar to traditional financial markets.

There are buyers.

There are sellers.

Prices move.

Participants respond to new information.

Someone can purchase a position and potentially sell it later at a different price.

Research and analysis can influence decisions.

These similarities make it understandable that prediction market participation is sometimes discussed using the language of investing and trading.

But similarities in market mechanics do not make the underlying activities identical.

Consider traditional stock investing.

When someone purchases a share of stock, they generally acquire an ownership interest in a business. That business may own equipment, intellectual property, real estate, inventory, cash, or other assets. It may employ workers, sell products, provide services, and generate revenue.

If the business becomes more productive and profitable over time, the economic value associated with that ownership can potentially increase.

The investment is connected to an underlying enterprise.

Prediction market contracts work differently.

Suppose you purchase a Yes contract asking whether inflation will fall below a specified level by a particular date.

You do not own part of inflation.

You do not own the government agency publishing the inflation report.

You do not own a productive asset that can generate revenue indefinitely.

You own a contract whose value depends on how a defined question is resolved.

Once the event is resolved, the contract reaches its conclusion.

That distinction is significant.

Traditional investments can potentially produce value over long periods because the underlying assets or enterprises continue existing. An event contract is generally designed around a finite outcome.

This does not mean traditional investing is safe.

Companies fail.

Stocks decline.

Real estate loses value.

Bonds can default.

Financial markets contain plenty of uncertainty.

The difference is not that investing contains risk while prediction markets do not.

The difference is partly about **what produces the return**.

With a productive business, financial returns can ultimately be connected to economic activity such as profits, cash flows, and growth.

With an event contract, the potential payout comes from the contract's resolution and market structure.

Prediction markets may more closely resemble financial trading when participants buy contracts with the intention of selling them before settlement.

Imagine a contract trading at $0.30.

A participant believes upcoming information will increase the market's estimate of the event's probability.

They purchase the contract.

Several days later, the price rises to $0.50.

They sell.

The underlying event has not occurred yet. The participant profited from the movement in the contract's market price.

That looks much more like **short-term trading**.

The participant was not necessarily trying to own something for years. They were attempting to identify a price discrepancy and profit when the market repriced the contract.

Financial traders do similar things in stocks, currencies, commodities, derivatives, and other markets.

But again, similarity does not mean equivalence.

The underlying instruments, regulations, risks, market structures, and sources of value can be very different.

This is why calling prediction markets "investing" without qualification can create confusion.

The word investing often carries associations with long-term wealth building, ownership, compounding, and productive assets.

Prediction market contracts do not automatically provide those characteristics.

A person can certainly allocate capital to them with the goal of earning a return.

But putting money into something does not, by itself, make that activity traditional investing.

What They Share With Sportsbooks, Wagering, and Gambling

Now consider the other side of the comparison.

Suppose someone is presented with the following question:

Will Team A win tonight's game?

They put money on Yes.

If Team A wins, they receive a financial payoff.

If Team A loses, they lose the amount risked.

Most people would immediately recognize the resemblance to sports betting.

Changing the interface from a betting slip to a market-style contract does not make that resemblance disappear.

This becomes even more obvious when prediction markets offer contracts involving sports, awards, entertainment, competitions, or other events commonly associated with wagering.

But the comparison extends beyond the subject of the event.

At its core, **gambling involves risking something of value on an uncertain outcome in hopes of receiving a larger amount of value**.

Many prediction market transactions can fit comfortably within that broad description.

You put money at risk.

An uncertain event occurs.

Your financial result depends on that outcome.

That does not mean prediction markets function exactly like every form of gambling.

A traditional sportsbook, for example, commonly establishes odds and accepts wagers under its own structure. A market-based system may instead allow participants to trade contracts with prices influenced by buying and selling activity.

Those differences can affect pricing and how participants interact with the market.

But from the perspective of the person risking money, the similarities remain important.

Imagine two people.

Person A places $100 on a sporting event through a sportsbook because they believe Team A will win.

Person B purchases $100 worth of prediction market contracts tied to Team A winning because they believe the same thing.

The mechanisms may differ.

The financial motivation may be nearly identical.

Both are risking money on an uncertain sporting outcome in hopes of receiving more money if their prediction proves correct.

Calling one "trading" and the other "betting" does not automatically create a meaningful economic difference for the participant.

This is why terminology should not distract you from what is actually happening to your money.

Prediction markets can also produce some of the same behavioral patterns associated with gambling.

Frequent participation can make each individual transaction feel less significant.

Winning can encourage larger positions.

Losses can encourage attempts to recover money quickly.

Exciting or emotionally important events can encourage people to abandon careful probability estimates and simply choose the outcome they want to happen.

The speed of certain markets can intensify this behavior.

If contracts are constantly available across politics, economics, sports, entertainment, and other subjects, there may always be another prediction available.

That availability can turn a tool for forecasting or speculation into continuous wagering for some participants.

There is also a psychological difference between asking:

"Is this contract attractively priced?"

and asking:

"Who do I think will win?"

The first question encourages analysis of price and probability.

The second can easily become a simple bet on an outcome.

This is particularly important when someone chooses contracts based primarily on personal preference.

Suppose a person strongly supports a particular candidate.

They purchase contracts predicting that candidate will win.

Their political preference does not provide evidence that the contract is underpriced.

The same applies to sports.

Being a devoted supporter of a team does not create a forecasting advantage.

Emotional attachment may actually make objective analysis more difficult.

This is where prediction markets can blur the line between informed speculation and entertainment-based wagering.

The contract itself does not force the participant to conduct research.

Someone can carefully model probabilities.

Someone else can click Yes because they like the outcome.

Both can participate in the same market.

Why the Same Event Contract Can Serve Very Different

Purposes Depending on How It Is Used

This brings us to perhaps the most useful way to think about prediction markets.

Instead of asking only:

"What is a prediction market?"

also ask:

"What is this person using the prediction market for?"

The answer can change how we understand the activity.

Consider a hypothetical contract asking whether a major hurricane will make landfall in a particular region before a specified date.

One participant might purchase the contract because they have studied weather forecasts and believe the market is underestimating the probability.

Their objective is speculative profit.

Another participant might purchase the contract because they find weather prediction entertaining and want a small amount of money riding on their forecast.

Their objective is entertainment.

A researcher might not purchase anything. They may simply observe the market price as one source of information about collective expectations.

Their objective is forecasting.

Now imagine a business whose financial performance could be harmed by the specified event. In certain circumstances, someone might consider an appropriate event-linked position as a way of partially offsetting financial exposure to an unfavorable outcome.

That would resemble hedging.

Same general market.

Very different purposes.

This is why **intent and economic function** matter.

A hammer can be used to build a house or break a window. Understanding what a tool is capable of does not tell you how someone will use it.

Prediction markets are similar.

The existence of legitimate forecasting or risk-management applications does not mean every person purchasing a contract is investing.

Likewise, the existence of gambling-like behavior does not mean prediction markets have no informational value.

Several things can be true at once.

A prediction market can aggregate expectations.

It can provide useful information.

It can offer opportunities for speculation.

It can potentially be used in certain risk-management situations.

And it can also be used simply to wager money on uncertain events.

These possibilities are not mutually exclusive.

This is why the question in the title of this book deliberately includes three possibilities:

Investing, speculation, or gambling?

For many ordinary participants, speculation may be the most useful middle category to consider.

A speculator commits capital because they believe an uncertain future development will move in their favor.

That description fits many prediction market participants reasonably well.

They are not necessarily purchasing a productive asset for long-term ownership.

They are taking a position based on what they believe will happen.

But even "speculation" can become too generous a description if no meaningful analysis is taking place.

Suppose someone opens a prediction market, sees ten contracts, and chooses outcomes based entirely on instinct.

They have no probability estimates.

They do not compare price with potential return.

They have no reason to believe the contracts are mispriced.

They simply hope to win.

Calling that sophisticated financial speculation because it happens on a market interface would be misleading.

It is much closer to gambling behavior.

On the other hand, suppose someone specializes in a particular type of economic data.

They carefully estimate probabilities, track their predictions, compare their estimates with market prices, avoid positions where they cannot identify an advantage, and risk only limited capital.

Their behavior looks much more like disciplined speculation.

The underlying contract may be identical.

The process is different.

Even disciplined speculation, however, should not automatically be confused with long-term investing.

The person is still attempting to profit from uncertainty.

This distinction matters because labels influence behavior.

If someone thinks:

"I am gambling $100 on this election,"

they may immediately recognize that losing the entire $100 is possible.

If the same person thinks:

"I am investing $100 in the election market,"

the word investing may make the activity feel more financially responsible than it actually is.

The dollars do not care what label you use.

The contract's payout does not change because you call yourself an investor.

The probability of the outcome does not improve because you describe the transaction as a trade.

A useful test is to remove the terminology completely.

Ask:

What am I purchasing?

What determines whether I make money?

What determines whether I lose money?

What evidence suggests the price is attractive?

How long will my money be exposed?

What happens if my prediction is wrong?

Why am I doing this instead of using the money somewhere else?

Those questions reveal far more than the label.

They also prepare us for the final major question of this book.

Even if prediction markets can be understood, analyzed, and sometimes used intelligently, why should an ordinary person participate at all?

That is a separate question from whether participation can produce profits.

An opportunity to make money is not automatically a reason to risk money.

Last Thoughts

Prediction markets do not fit perfectly into a single financial category because the same type of contract can be used for very different purposes. Their market prices and trading mechanics can resemble financial trading, their search for mispriced probabilities can resemble speculation, and their dependence on uncertain outcomes can closely resemble wagering and gambling. The most useful approach is therefore not to become overly attached to a label, but to examine what is actually happening to the participant's money and why the position exists. That leads directly to the most practical question in this entire book: even if you understand prediction markets, **what is the point of participating?** In the next chapter, we will examine whether speculation, forecasting, hedging, entertainment, or potential profit provides a compelling reason to put money into these markets at all.

Chapter 6: What Is the Point of Participating?

Understanding how prediction markets work does not automatically provide a reason to participate in them. This distinction is especially important because financial products and market-based platforms can create the impression that activity itself is productive. Seeing prices move, researching outcomes, and successfully predicting events can feel financially sophisticated, but none of those things answer the most basic question: **Why should you put your money here at all?** For some people, prediction markets may serve a specific purpose. For others, the potential reward may not justify the uncertainty, effort, or opportunity cost. Before treating prediction markets as part of a financial strategy, it is worth examining what participants are actually trying to accomplish and whether another use of their money could accomplish that goal more effectively.

Speculation, Forecasting, Hedging, Entertainment, and Other Reasons People Participate

People enter prediction markets for different reasons, and those reasons matter.

One of the most obvious is speculation.

A participant believes a contract is incorrectly priced, purchases a position, and hopes to profit if their assessment proves more accurate than the market's.

We have explored this throughout the book.

But speculation is only one reason prediction markets exist.

Another is **forecasting**.

Prediction markets can provide information about what groups of participants collectively expect to happen. Someone interested in an election, economic announcement, policy decision, or another uncertain event may watch the market without ever purchasing a contract.

In this situation, the prediction market is functioning as an information source rather than an investment opportunity.

That is an important distinction.

You can find prediction markets useful without putting a single dollar into them.

Suppose you are interested in whether a particular economic outcome will occur.

You could look at professional forecasts.

You could examine historical data.

You could read research.

You could look at surveys.

And you could observe a prediction market to see how participants are collectively pricing the outcome.

The market becomes another piece of information.

There is no requirement that you trade simply because you are looking at the prices.

This may actually be one of the most overlooked uses of prediction markets. Public attention often focuses on who won money, who made an impressive prediction, or how much a contract moved. But the market's informational function can be useful independently of participation.

Another possible purpose is hedging, which we introduced in the previous chapter.

A **hedge** is a position intended to reduce the financial impact of another risk.

Imagine a simplified hypothetical situation involving a business whose revenue could be substantially affected by a particular measurable event.

If an appropriate market existed, a position that produced a payout when that unfavorable event occurred could potentially offset some of the business's losses.

The purpose would not necessarily be:

"I hope this happens so I can make money."

The reasoning could instead be:

"If this happens, I will lose money somewhere else, so this position may partially reduce the financial damage."

That is fundamentally different from purchasing a contract because you think an outcome will occur and want to profit from it.

But hedging should not be treated as a universal justification for prediction market participation.

Most ordinary participants are unlikely to have a natural financial exposure that perfectly corresponds with a particular event contract. A poorly designed hedge can also create additional risks rather than reducing them.

Another major reason people participate is simpler:

Entertainment.

There is nothing complicated about that motivation.

Some people enjoy predicting outcomes.

Putting a small amount of money behind a prediction can make watching an event more exciting.

Sports betting has long demonstrated this appeal. Fantasy competitions, office pools, and other prediction-based activities appeal to similar interests.

Prediction markets can satisfy that desire across a much broader collection of subjects.

A person who closely follows politics may enjoy testing their election predictions.

Someone interested in economics may enjoy forecasting government reports.

Someone interested in entertainment may enjoy predicting awards.

Someone interested in sports may enjoy event contracts related to games or championships.

If entertainment is the real purpose, it is useful to acknowledge that honestly.

There is no need to rename entertainment spending as investing to make it sound more sophisticated.

Someone might spend $30 going to the movies.

Another person might spend $30 at an amusement park.

Someone else might decide that risking $30 on predictions is entertaining.

The financial question becomes whether that person can comfortably afford to lose the money being used for entertainment.

This is very different from saying:

"I am putting this $30 here because I expect it to help build long-term wealth."

The same transaction can feel different once the purpose is stated clearly.

There are also people who participate because they want to test their forecasting ability.

Money can create accountability.

It is easy to say:

"I knew that was going to happen."

It is harder to consistently record your probability estimates before events occur and evaluate them afterward.

Prediction markets can provide a financial version of that feedback.

But once again, someone does not necessarily need to risk significant money to improve their forecasting skills.

The existence of a purpose does not automatically justify the size of the financial commitment.

That principle will remain important as we consider whether prediction markets deserve a place in someone's broader financial life.

Comparing the Potential Reward With Simply Keeping or Using the Money Elsewhere

Whenever money is committed to one opportunity, it cannot simultaneously be used for something else.

This creates **opportunity cost**.

Suppose you have $500 available.

You could put it into prediction market contracts.

But you could also keep the money.

You could use it to pay an upcoming expense.

You could reduce debt.

You could put it toward education or training.

You could invest it in a business.

You could purchase equipment that helps you earn income.

You could use it for another financial asset.

Or you could simply maintain the cash because having accessible money provides value of its own.

The correct choice will differ from person to person.

The important point is that prediction markets do not compete against nothing.

They compete against every other possible use of the money.

This changes how potential returns should be evaluated.

Imagine you are considering risking $500 to potentially make $75.

The question should not only be:

"Would I like to make $75?"

Of course you would.

A more useful question is:

"Is the possibility of making $75 worth exposing $500 to this particular risk?"

Then another:

"What else could I do with that $500?"

And another:

"How much time will I spend researching and managing this position?"

These questions can make an apparently attractive opportunity look very different.

Suppose you spend fifteen hours researching several markets and ultimately earn $40.

You made money.

But if your goal was purely financial, the return should be considered alongside the time and effort required to generate it.

This is particularly important for beginners who become fascinated with finding an informational edge.

Research can become endless.

You might spend hours reading economic reports, studying polling data, watching news, comparing forecasts, and monitoring contract prices.

There is nothing inherently wrong with that if you enjoy the process.

But if the objective is to generate income, the value of your time matters.

A person who earns $100 after spending fifty hours researching markets technically earned a profit.

Whether that was an effective financial activity is a separate question.

Capital also has value because of what it allows you to do.

Having $1,000 available can provide flexibility.

It can help cover an unexpected expense.

It can allow you to purchase something necessary without borrowing.

It can provide capital for an opportunity that appears later.

Putting that $1,000 into uncertain event contracts changes what the money can do for you while it is committed.

This is why **doing nothing is a legitimate financial decision**.

Financial culture often makes inactivity sound like failure.

People are encouraged to make their money work, find opportunities, enter markets, and maximize returns.

But not every available opportunity deserves capital.

You do not need to participate in every market you understand.

You do not need to place a trade because you have an opinion.

You do not need to monetize every prediction.

Sometimes keeping your money is the better decision.

Prediction markets can make this particularly difficult because humans naturally form opinions about future events.

You may already believe Candidate A will win.

You may already believe interest rates will change.

You may already believe Team A will win.

Then you discover that a market will allow you to put money behind that opinion.

The existence of the market creates an opportunity to act.

But your opinion existed before the financial opportunity.

Ask yourself whether attaching money to that opinion actually improves your financial position.

Sometimes the answer may be yes.

Sometimes the answer may be no.

And "no" is not a failure to recognize an opportunity.

It can simply be a recognition that the potential reward does not justify the risk.

Deciding Whether Prediction Markets Have a Legitimate Place in Your Personal Financial Strategy

We can now return to the question that motivated this entire book.

What is the point of investing in prediction markets?

The answer may be that "**investing" is not always the best way to describe what you are doing**.

If you are purchasing event contracts because you believe the market has mispriced an outcome, you may be engaging primarily in speculation.

If you are using a contract to offset a genuine financial exposure, you may be hedging.

If you are risking a small amount because predicting an event makes it more entertaining, you may essentially be wagering for entertainment.

If you are simply watching market prices to understand collective expectations, you are using the prediction market as a forecasting tool and may not need to risk money at all.

Those distinctions should influence how prediction markets fit into a personal financial strategy.

Someone trying to build long-term wealth should be particularly careful about assuming that prediction market participation serves the same purpose as owning productive assets over long periods.

An event contract eventually resolves.

There is no business continuing to operate afterward.

There are no future earnings from the contract.

There is no long-term compounding within the resolved position.

You were right, wrong, or you exited before settlement.

Then the position is finished.

To continue generating returns through prediction markets, you generally need to continue finding new opportunities.

That creates a very different process from purchasing an asset intended to produce value over many years.

This does not automatically make prediction market participation bad.

It makes its purpose different.

A person who understands that distinction can make a more deliberate decision about how much, if any, money should be allocated to it.

One useful question is:

What financial job am I asking this money to perform?

If the money is intended for an essential expense, risking it on uncertain events would create an obvious conflict with that purpose.

If the money represents capital you cannot comfortably lose, prediction markets may be an inappropriate place for it.

If the money is intended for entertainment and you are genuinely comfortable losing it, the decision has a different context.

If the money is speculative capital and you have a clear reason to believe you possess an advantage, prediction markets may represent one of several speculative opportunities you could evaluate.

The important part is matching the risk to the purpose.

You should also consider whether prediction market participation is improving or damaging your financial behavior.

Are you researching carefully?

Are you tracking how much money is actually at risk?

Are you evaluating results over meaningful periods rather than celebrating individual wins?

Can you walk away from a market when the price is unattractive?

Can you accept a loss without immediately trying to recover it?

Can you see an interesting contract and decide not to participate?

That final ability may be one of the most important.

A market constantly offers decisions.

You do not have to make all of them.

If you cannot observe an event contract without feeling compelled to take a position, the activity may no longer be serving a thoughtful financial purpose.

Prediction markets should not turn every uncertain event in life into an opportunity to risk money.

There will always be another election.

Another economic report.

Another sporting event.

Another announcement.

Another question about the future.

The ability to bet or trade on those outcomes does not create an obligation to do so.

This brings us to a more balanced understanding of prediction markets.

They can be fascinating information systems.

They can provide a mechanism for people to express different probability estimates through market prices.

They can create opportunities for disciplined speculation.

They may have certain hedging applications.

They can also function as entertainment and, depending on how they are used, closely resemble gambling.

None of these realities requires you to participate.

Understanding the market gives you something more valuable than a prediction.

It gives you the ability to decide whether the market deserves your money in the first place.

Last Thoughts

Prediction markets can serve legitimate purposes, but those purposes are not the same for every participant. Some people speculate on mispriced probabilities, some observe the markets for forecasting information, some may use particular contracts to manage risk, and others participate primarily for entertainment. The important question is not whether money can be made. Money can potentially be made through many risky activities. The better question is whether the expected reward, time commitment, uncertainty, and possibility of loss make prediction markets a sensible use of **your capital**. There is nothing contradictory about finding prediction markets interesting while deciding not to put money into them. Understanding a financial opportunity does not require participating in it.

Last Thoughts: Understanding the Market Before Risking Your Money

Prediction markets can make uncertainty feel unusually concrete. Instead of simply wondering whether something will happen, you can see a price, take a position, and attach real money to your belief. That structure can make prediction markets useful for understanding collective expectations, interesting for people who enjoy forecasting, and potentially profitable for participants who can identify genuine differences between market prices and reasonable probability estimates. But none of those qualities make prediction markets automatically appropriate for your money. The most important lesson from this book is not how to predict the future. It is how to recognize **what you are actually doing when you put money behind a prediction**.

Prediction Markets Are Tools, Not Guaranteed Opportunities

Prediction markets are ultimately tools for putting prices on uncertain outcomes.

Like many financial tools, what matters is how they are used.

A participant might use a market to speculate on an outcome they believe has been incorrectly priced. Another person might observe the same market because they are interested in what participants collectively expect to happen. Someone else might participate primarily because they enjoy having money attached to their predictions.

The existence of a market does not mean an opportunity exists for you.

This is worth emphasizing because prediction markets can create the appearance of constant opportunity.

There may always be another contract available.

One market resolves and another appears. An election ends, but another political event is approaching. An economic report is released, but another report is coming. One sporting event finishes and another begins.

If you approach prediction markets with the assumption that you should always have money somewhere, the availability of contracts can encourage unnecessary activity.

But a market being available does not mean its price is attractive.

Suppose you examine a contract and estimate that an outcome has approximately a 60 percent probability of occurring.

The contract is trading around $0.60.

You may conclude that the market is priced reasonably close to your own estimate.

There may be nothing to do.

That is a perfectly legitimate conclusion.

You do not need to manufacture an advantage simply because you want to participate.

The same principle applies when you do not understand the event well enough to estimate its probability.

Imagine seeing a contract connected to a complicated economic announcement.

You understand the basic question, but you do not understand the economic variables well enough to determine whether the market's price is reasonable.

You can skip it.

Prediction markets do not reward participation itself.

They reward favorable financial outcomes, and those outcomes are never guaranteed.

Even an apparent advantage can disappear because your probability estimate was wrong, new information emerged, the market moved before you acted, or the event produced an unexpected result.

This is why the idea of a **guaranteed prediction market opportunity** should immediately be treated with skepticism.

Probability and guarantees do not belong comfortably together.

An event can be extremely likely without being certain.

A contract can appear dramatically mispriced while your analysis is missing something.

A long winning streak can end.

An unexpected event can occur.

The risk does not disappear because a participant feels confident.

This also means that prediction markets should not be viewed as machines that convert research into guaranteed profits.

Research can improve decision-making.

It cannot eliminate uncertainty.

Someone can spend days studying an event and still lose money.

That is not necessarily evidence that research was useless. It is evidence that uncertainty remained.

The healthiest way to understand prediction markets is therefore as tools.

They can display changing expectations.

They can facilitate speculation.

They can create financial exposure to defined events.

They can sometimes serve other purposes, including entertainment or particular forms of risk management.

But a tool does not automatically deserve your money simply because you understand how to use it.

Understanding Something Does Not Mean You Need to Participate in It

Financial education sometimes creates an unintended pressure to act.

You learn how a market works.

You understand the terminology.

You become comfortable reading prices.

Then it can feel natural to think:

"Now I should try it."

But knowledge and participation are two different things.

You can understand real estate without purchasing property.

You can understand options without trading options.

You can understand cryptocurrency without owning cryptocurrency.

And you can understand prediction markets without purchasing event contracts.

In fact, understanding prediction markets may give you more reasons to avoid certain contracts than to purchase them.

Before reading this book, a contract priced at $0.90 might have looked like an easy opportunity to make ten cents.

Now you understand that you may be risking substantially more than you can potentially gain.

A contract priced at $0.15 might once have looked cheap.

Now you recognize that a low price may simply reflect a low estimated probability of success.

A contract moving rapidly upward might once have created a fear of missing out.

Now you understand that entering after the market has already incorporated new information may leave you paying a price that offers little advantage.

That is financial education working properly.

The goal is not necessarily to make you more active.

Sometimes the result of becoming more knowledgeable is deciding to do less.

This is particularly important with prediction markets because having opinions about future events is normal.

You probably already make predictions without thinking about them.

You expect certain economic conditions.

You think a particular team will win.

You believe a political event will unfold a certain way.

You expect a technology to become more popular.

Prediction markets create the possibility of attaching money to those opinions.

But **having an opinion does not create a financial obligation**.

You do not need to monetize everything you believe.

This distinction becomes even more important when the prediction involves something you care deeply about.

Political preferences can become positions.

Sports loyalties can become positions.

Personal beliefs about the economy can become positions.

Once money becomes attached, it can become harder to separate what you want to happen from what the evidence suggests is likely to happen.

Sometimes the best financial decision is to remain an observer.

You can watch a prediction market change as information arrives.

You can compare the market's probabilities with your own expectations.

You can study why participants were right or wrong.

You can use the market to learn about probability and forecasting.

None of that requires risking money.

There is also no prize for participating in the greatest number of financial markets.

Personal finance is not a collection game.

You do not need stocks, real estate, cryptocurrency, commodities, prediction markets, collectibles, and every other available financial instrument simply because each one exists.

Every additional activity requires some combination of money, attention, knowledge, and risk tolerance.

Those resources are limited.

Choosing what not to participate in can therefore be just as important as choosing what to participate in.

Making an Informed Decision About Whether the Risk Is Worthwhile

After everything we have covered, the final decision becomes personal.

Is participating in prediction markets worthwhile for you?

There is no universal answer.

Instead, you can return to several questions developed throughout this book.

Start with the simplest:

Why am I doing this?

If the answer is entertainment, acknowledge that.

If the answer is speculation, acknowledge that.

If the answer is forecasting, ask whether you actually need to risk money to accomplish that goal.

If the answer is hedging, identify the specific financial exposure the contract is intended to offset.

If the answer is investing, examine whether the activity really serves the financial purpose you normally associate with investing.

Clear language makes clear decisions easier.

Then consider the money itself.

How much are you actually willing to lose?

Not how much do you expect to lose.

How much could disappear without interfering with your financial responsibilities or forcing you to make decisions you would otherwise avoid?

Those are different questions.

A participant may believe there is only a 10 percent chance of losing a position.

The financial consequences of that 10 percent outcome still matter.

Probability does not make a loss less real when the unlikely outcome occurs.

Next, consider your reason for believing the contract is attractive.

If your answer is:

"I just think it will happen,"

you have identified your prediction.

You have not necessarily identified a financial advantage.

A more complete explanation would consider the probability you assign to the outcome, the price available, the potential payout, the amount at risk, and the possibility that your estimate is wrong.

You should also consider how you behave after money is committed.

Can you change your mind when new information contradicts your position?

Can you accept that a loss has occurred without immediately trying to recover it?

Can you reduce a position when your original reasoning no longer makes sense?

Can you stop after winning?

Can you decide that today's available markets offer nothing worth purchasing?

These behavioral questions matter because financial risk is not created only by the contracts.

It can also be created by the participant.

A disciplined strategy can become reckless when position sizes increase.

Research can become confirmation bias when contrary information is ignored.

Speculation can become gambling behavior when the purpose shifts from finding favorable opportunities to constantly needing another prediction.

The transition may happen gradually.

That is why the central question should remain visible:

Is the potential reward worth the risk I am taking?

Not whether the event is exciting.

Not whether you strongly believe you are right.

Not whether someone online made a large profit.

Not whether the market is popular.

And not whether the activity is described as investing, trading, speculation, or betting.

What matters is what happens to your money.

Prediction markets can be useful, fascinating, and intellectually challenging without being necessary components of a personal financial strategy.

For some people, limited and deliberate participation may make sense within the purpose they have defined for it.

For others, observation may provide nearly everything they find valuable about prediction markets without exposing their money to uncertain outcomes.

And for some people, the best conclusion may simply be:

"I understand how this works, but I do not see a good enough reason to put my money into it."

That is an informed financial decision too.

Last Thoughts

Prediction markets turn uncertainty into something that can be priced and traded, but they do not eliminate the uncertainty itself. Throughout this book, we have seen that making money requires more than predicting the correct outcome. Price matters. Probability matters. Risk matters. Costs matter. Behavior matters. And perhaps most importantly, the purpose of participating matters. Whether you ultimately view prediction markets as investing, speculation, gambling, forecasting tools, or some combination of these depends partly on how they are being used. Whatever label you choose, the standard for risking your money should remain the same: **understand what you are buying, understand what you can lose, understand why you are participating, and decide whether the potential reward genuinely justifies the risk.**

About the Author

Roggie "Raj" Clark is an entrepreneur and a 10-year marketing professional with a proven track record in e-commerce and digital business growth. Having built and managed successful online stores with thousands of sales and consulted for numerous marketing clients, Roggie has mastered the intricacies of online marketing, branding, and consumer behavior. He has also written several popular books on digital marketing, SEO (search engine optimization), and programming (HTML, CSS, and JavaScript).

As a former marketing manager at a fintech company—a role he secured through his own marketing and financial expertise—Roggie gained firsthand experience in financial strategy and wealth-building. This journey inspired him to share insights with amateur investors, helping them save money, make smarter financial decisions, and build long-term wealth. Raj currently lives in Maryland with his sister and niece.

www.ingramcontent.com/pod-product-compliance
Lightning Source LLC
LaVergne TN
LVHW050823061126
851857LV00012B/954
9798256286309